I0896579

salmonpoetry

Publishing Irish & International Poetry Since 1981

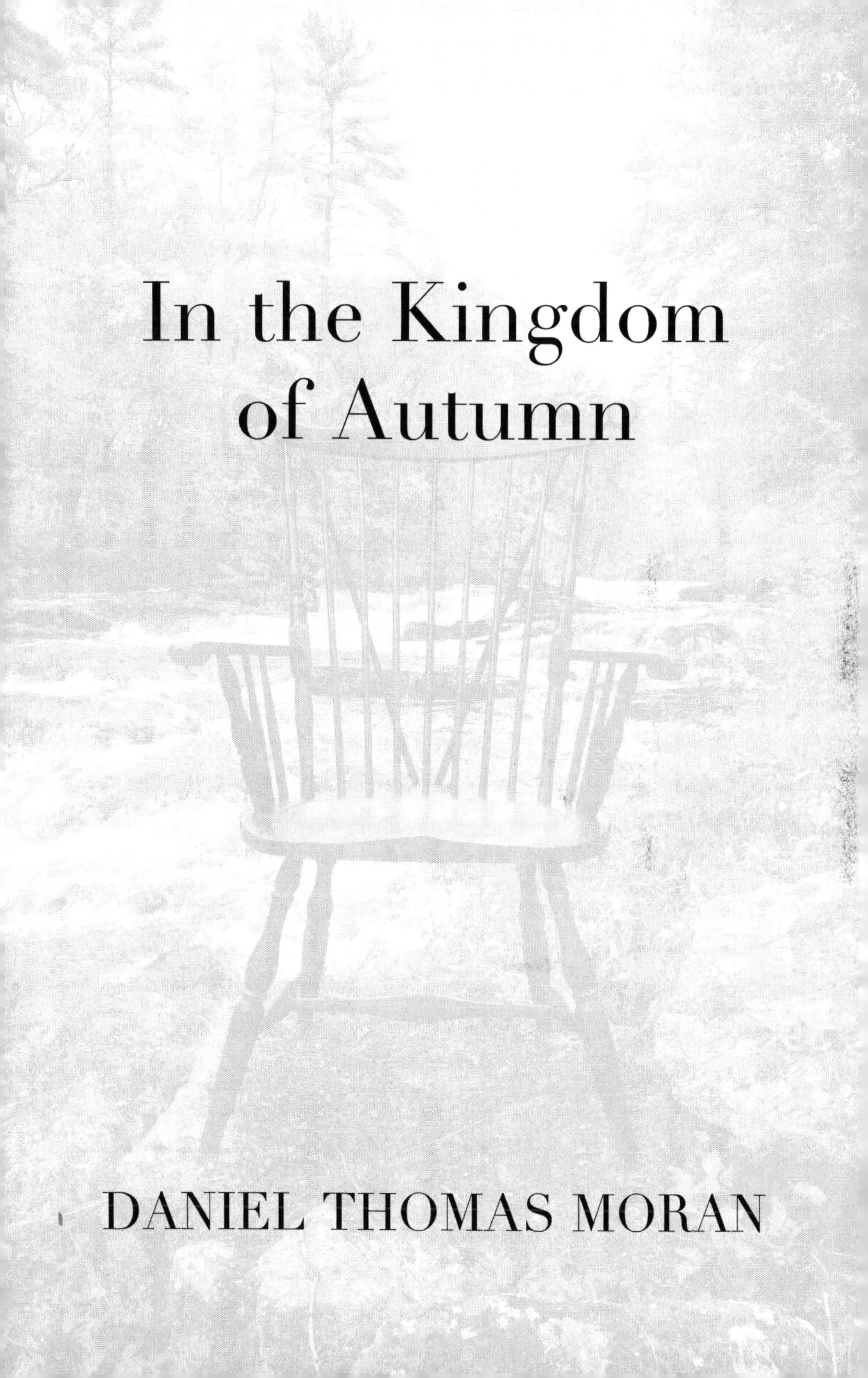

In the Kingdom of Autumn

DANIEL THOMAS MORAN

This collection is published in 2020 by
Salmon Poetry, Cliffs of Moher, County Clare, Ireland
www.salmonpoetry.com e: info@salmonpoetry.com

ISBN 978-1-912561-82-7

Cover & Title Page Image: *Photograph by the author of his handmade Windsor chair, against the backdrop of the Warner River, New Hampshire, USA*

Cover Design & Typesetting: *Siobhán Hutson*

Printed in Ireland by Sprint Print

This book is dedicated with love to my son Gregory Riordan
and, as always, to Karen

Acknowledgments

Some of the poems is this collection have been previously published in the following journals: *Poetry Salzburg Review* (Austria), *The Humanist, Columbia Journal, Contemporary Literature Review India, Exit 13, Hektoen International, Here in the Afterlife* (2017 Integral Contemporary Literature Press (Bucharest, Romania), *FEKT* (Kosovo), *Journal of The Visuality and Mathematics Conference (Belgrade, Serbia), The Henniker Review, Ekphrasis Project-Joost de Jonge* (Amsterdam, The Netherlands), *Journal of Dental Humanities, Levure Litteraire* (Paris, France), *Like Light: 25 Years of Poetry and Prose* (Bright Hill Press), *Lit.Cat, Literary Matters – The Journal of The Association of Literary Scholars, Critics and Writers, Even the Daybreak: 35 Years of Salmon Poetry 35th Anniversary Anthology* (Salmon Poetry, Ireland), *The Same, New Contrast: South African Literary Journal, Universal Oneness: An Anthology of Magnum Opus Poems From Around The World* (India) and *VIA: Voices in Italian Americana* (Bordighera Press).

The water you touch in a river is the last of that which has passed, and the first of that which is coming. Thus it is with time present. Life, if well spent, is long.

Leonardo da Vinci

Contents

Foreword

I've written a trio of detective novels but never solved how to write a poem. As a young writer (many, many years ago), I read a lot of poets, was in awe of a few (Dante and T.S. Eliot in particular), loved some (Whitman, Dickinson, Frost, Hopkins, Auden come to mind), and was inspired to make several attempts. I eventually incinerated the embarrassing results and scattered the ashes to avoid them ever being found.

I turned to writing novels because it freed me from the constraint and precision that, in my view, poetry demands. In the confinement of a poem, the awkward and amateurish call attention to themselves. The capacious nature of a novel is far more forgiving. With a novel you can let loose, detour and digress, pursue multiple story lines, wander down alleys and byways. (If I sound defensive, well, my first novel was over six hundred pages.)

Knowing I could never write poetry didn't kill my appetite for reading it. But over time my interest was diminished, if not extinguished, by a growing body of poetry I found obscure and self-indulgent. Too often, the introspective quickly descended into the impenetrable. Like those scholars of old who labored to decipher Egyptian hieroglyphs before the unearthing of the Rosetta Stone, I was stymied by texts whose meaning I couldn't unlock.

Daniel Thomas Moran restored my faith. I came upon him via the serendipity of geography. For many years my family summered on Shelter Island, a once-obscure, idyllic, intricately insular fishing and farming community nestled in Peconic Bay, on the East End of Long Island, New York, that has since morphed into yet another favored playground of the poohbahs of high finance and fashion.

Beset by a problem tooth, I asked around about dentists on the island. A friend recommended one whom she described a "terrific poet as well as top-rated dentist." At first, I thought she was kidding. Among the words dentist brought to mind--cavity, pain, fear—poetry wasn't one. The artistry and aesthetic of poetry seemed to me far removed from the grinding and repairing of teeth. Only later would I be reminded that the creative genius of Wallace Stevens (insurance executive) and William Carlos Williams (physician) lay in part in their distance from the cookie-cutter orthodoxies of the academy.

I decided on an off-island, un-poetic dentist whose sole concentration, I imagined, would be on my tooth. As it turned out, I was left for long periods staring at the TV mounted on her wall while she consulted her computer on the furious fluctuations in her stock portfolio. Yet I remained curious about the dentist with the poetic bent, and my friend enthusiastically endowed me with a book of Moran's poems titled Sheltered by Islands.

I instantly discovered that Daniel Thomas Moran was no amateur aspirant but a fully formed, visionary artist with a unique poetic voice. Moran's poetry never confuses the profound with the pretentious. It reminds us that life has no need to be transcended. Its higher meaning surrounds us in lowly things, in trees and bays and stonewalls, in the ordinary moments and everyday places in which we love and mate and break each other's hearts.

I have neither the learning nor chutzpah to match one poet against another. Yet my deep admiration for Moran's poetry is rooted in the same earth as other poets who mean much to me. Moran's direct, unpretentious use of language recalls Emily Dickinson's stripped-down, open-eyed, unsparing ability to find within a simple rose an estate in Sicily. He shares the American aspiration to strike the chords of a common humanity that inspired Walt Whitman to sing and drove Allen Ginsberg to howl. (Like Whitman, Moran spent a part of his life in Suffolk County, where he was named the county's poet laureate.)

As poet and chair maker (and, I suppose, dentist), Moran is a craftsman, a master of the tools of his trade(s). "A poem is a chair," he tells us, "a chair a poem./Don't ask me to explain./I have built/both with only/my bare hands." Moran's poems are the well-built product of an experienced artisan. But they display more than the skillful use of tools. In his hands, they move beyond craft to art. They are infused with the singular intelligence and ineffable genius that the artist alone possesses.

As well as practice dentistry, Moran has been a faculty member in a distinguished university. But it's obvious that his true vocation is as a poet. He is in love with words. He makes them wink and weep and sparkle. I was struck by the reach and richness of his art from the moment I opened In the Kingdom of Autumn and consulted the table of contents. The first entries read to me like a Moran-esque haiku: "My Farmer's Daughter/A Poem and a Chair/ Seven Days in Cuba/Falling/ Psychotherapy/ The Dreaming of Cats."

Chronicler and celebrant of the beauty, meaning, and passion that live deep within the proximate and familiar, Daniel Thomas Moran invites us to open our eyes. He teaches us to see with a new clarity and freshness. While most of us compose our thoughts in sentences and paragraphs, he thinks in poetry. It's who he is. How fortunate we are to have him.

PETER QUINN

In the Kingdom of Autumn

Waiting in New Orleans

for Karen

I recall with soft clarity
the spring day we traveled,
together and briefly,
that tiny voyage from
Shelter Island to Sag Harbor.
Side by side in our automobiles,
we chatted only a few sentences
through rolled down windows.
We both bore the long and
lingering scents of mourning.

You asked where it was I
might be headed that morning.
I said to New Orleans to
see an old friend.

On a dappled side street in
the French Quarter, through
a window populated with odd
trappings of voodoo and souvenirs,
I found a crudely carved angel
in a long orange dress,
embroidered with painted stars,
which I carried home again.

I hung it high up
above my window,
letting it float over me, in
a room I would use to sit.
I hoped it might watch me,
through many long days when
no one was watching.

Now, years later, we sit
side by side in our home,
far from ferries and short voyages,
far from accumulated sadness, in
a place of rivers and mountains,
where angels live among
tall trees and moss-coated stones.

My angel has become
our angel, pitched slightly forward,
high above a new window which
looks out to a whispering paradise.

We no longer wander separate.
You no longer ask
where it is I am going. Now,
our chairs nested side by side,
Our dinner plates rest side by side,
We sleep side by side in
a bottomless contentment,
Free to forget that
we don't believe in angels.

My Farmer's Daughter

for Karen

She says she
hates the gardening,
but she loves the
new greens and all
their tender blossoms.
It is something like
how she hates the
winter, but loves the
magic that is snow, falling
and falling all afternoon.

In the autumn she
loves how the hills
slowly surrender to
the rising color, but
she is disquieted by all the
death, and the utterances
of loss expressed by the
drying crackle of litter.

Maybe it is
the steep recall in a
pain felt in the knees,
or how the soil
finds its way into
the swirl of a fingertip.
Maybe it's the short
light and deepening cold,
Maybe time spent to
fret over whether the
birds of our summer
are safe somewhere, and

Wondering through
many November days,
who is feeding nectar to
our ruby-throated children
on their long, long descent
down the hemisphere.

I remind her that
she is a farmer's daughter.
I remind her how once
she spent the long flat days
defying the Minnesota wind,
tending to pens filled with
eggs and white chickens.

And she explains
that it was her imagination
that came along to save her,
one purple day when she
was very young, and first
noticed that the sky was
a giant over her head, and
the roads in every direction
seemed to go the very
same place.

So, now we
are of that age when
complaint is a currency,
where nothing at all
seems the way we think
we remember it.

But, we have found
a place and it is ours,
where we must be grateful
for even January, and for
the line of black beneath
our nails, and the ache
in our knees which reminds
us we are alive, and that
the gardens we've made
beckon to be watered,
yet again.

A Poem and a Chair

for Peter Galbert

A poem is a chair,
a chair, a poem.
Don't ask me
to explain.

I have built
both with only
my bare hands,
so I know.

You will just
have to trust me.

If you wish me
to also say
that a painting
is a chair,

Or that a concerto
is a chair,
I will.
They are.

But, not like
a poem is a chair.

Have a seat.

Listen.

Seven Days in Cuba

Havana sleeps
under a cloak of
damp and darkness,
A rare light
fluoresces from a
window festooned
with Spanish iron.

The stars float softly
over a blue sea.
On ancient cobbles,
small dogs lie
in grateful prayer,
for the blessings of
a cool evening.

Regiments of Royal Palms
stand sentinel along
a stretch of sea wall.
In Cuba, the invader is
never far from the shore.

But, there is a sun
which pulls the hard sweet
from the mahogany soil,
The rum maker
crafting fragrant dreams
from the hard sweet.

Another dawn is
reason enough for a
song and celebration.
On every corner,
Tres, Guiro, and Bongos
pump out the dulcet
chords of the heart, the
rhythm of the street.

Cuba, he venido aquí
para decir que,
*no soy tu enemigo.**

* Cuba, I have come here to say that I am not your enemy.

Falling

for Peter Quinn

With time comes
the falling away,
of familiar touch,
fragrance through
an open window.

In the quietude,
we wonder about
the vigor of the wind,
some loose sounds
in the rafters.

To each thing
comes change.
In the graying days,
the sun becomes
an absent lover.

Yet in these years,
to those so disposed,
There is a peace
of curious quality,
a truce reluctantly signed.

The comforts of our
life's clichés shed
like old skin.

In the emptying bottle,
a sadness and yet,
the satisfied thirst.
Days age, while the
day retains its bloom.

And we can
only but wonder,
Will there be one
to take note
of our leaving?
And then, how
might we know?

Psychotherapy

No one ever
gets the parents
they deserve,

Born as
we are, with
empty bellies,
filled with insatiable
hankering.

Our childhoods,
become a bowl
of broth
with no meat,

All of it
seasoned with a
touch too much
pepper and brine.

Then, desperate,
we squander our
lives in search
of butter,

For all the
bread we never
had.

The Dreaming of Cats

for the Blackwater Veterinarians

Cats always look
comfortable,
Stretched against
a cool porch
floor,
Across a
square of afternoon
sun.

Tiptoeing
whispers
in their fur
slippers,
They flow
without effort
from bed to bowl
to bed.

Watching life
with a privileged
ennui,
They feel
accomplished at
how well they
endure us,
While snoozing
sixteen
hours of a
day.

We can
only imagine,
That they
inhabit vivid
dreams.
We wonder, as
they gently
twitch in
their profound
slumber,

Ears drawn
back tight,
Hunched into
the savannah
grasses,

Their eyes
cutting
through the dust
and blinding
heat.
They have
nothing if not
time.

They watch,
wound like a
fatal spring,
to fix on one
who looks
unsure,
then they
wait for them
to stray.

India

for Ankur and Khushbu

India is the kingdom
of a billion tiny efforts.
By wooden cart pushers, and
one-handed ditch carvers.
By rickety pedal cart climbers.
All those who dance with the traffic,
and the beggar with the basket of cobra.

In India little is spent, nothing wasted,
by them who feed all those who eat,
By the ones who coax the wells, and
those who scratch at the dry earth.
In India, even the dogs have their places,
Snarling for what little remains, or lying
out along the roads stretched in sleep.

In India there is always one more
tiny space which could be filled.
And though the air holds its weight, and
the passing waters weep their pain,
In India these are the holy places,
of all the many gods who keep watch,
over the conversations of men drinking tea.

India is the puttering three-wheeled taxis,
clotting the roundabouts and lanes.
The Indian men who fry Indian things,
Boiling the sacred water and the ghee
in their dented vessels and kettles.
The drivers of groaning buses steer
the travelers through the chaos.

India is the tiny hands of the thief-
children of the monkey-god, Hanuman.
All the lungs breathing of that blue smoke
which curls and lifts out of every crevice.
The bony shoulders of memory
that bear the soft weight of long silk drapes.
The ancient din outside the ancient walls.

India is carried on bicycles stacked
with burlap sacks, thin lengths of wood,
all that is precious, and all collected things.
India is the gathered pastel women
who reclaim the old bricks, while babies play.
Bald-headed loin-clothed holy men, and
dirty urchins who hawk ten rupee necklaces.
It is khaki policemen and palace guards, and
the monsoons of uniformed children
who pour from the doors of schools.
India is the old ladies stringing wedding garlands.
The bony-hipped cows grazing the trash.
The ten million machines with two wheels and three.
The sunrise always muted by yesterday's haze.

India is the overflowing trains, set
on endless miles of creaking rails,
conveying all things which must be
gotten from here to somewhere else.
For India must maintain its motions, and
its rare places of deep stillness, and all those
voices chanting mantra praises to the invisible.

And India is the magnificent marble mausoleums,
set among dilapidated shelters of the living.
India is the shop window teeming with brass,
and the pastels which color everything.
The crisp bleached linens of the mahogany old men,
and the mother whose babies are born hungering,
India is the bride whose groom arrives dancing.

Rockets

I am in my seat,
looking through the
reaching arms of giants,
that stand down along
the river's bank.
The sky is even
more blue, when set
behind the green
canopies of late July.

The news presents itself,
against a distant echo
of rumbling sound.
The breeze has animated.
The rushing waters have
gathered yesterday's rain.
The clouds seem alive.

But the news is insistent.
The suffering, echoes
off of these hillsides.
The images are of
screams and mourning,
rubble and lifeless bodies.

Why must we give in
to killing?
Why must all the heroes
be armed?
Why must all our beliefs
be carried on the
backs of rockets?

Oh, Danny Boy

My Mother named
me Daniel.
Like all names,
it has its
connotations.

It is actually a
Hebrew name.
It means
God is my judge.
But, I am not a Jew.
I also refuse to
be judged by any
gods, ever.

The first Daniel
earned his renown,
interpreting the dreams
of a king named
Nebuchadnezzar,
a name I am relieved
had gone out of fashion
by the spring of 1957.

Daniel also claimed
to foresee the
end of days.
I have foreseen them
as well, but have
chosen to not trouble
my mind about it.

The Irish,
of whom I am one,
say the name Daniel
means *attractive*.
That is my clan,
and a definition
much more
to my liking.

The Drums of Autumn

It is one of those
brilliant September days.
The choking damp and
the cloying heat that
were yesterday, have
been swept down
off the mountains
and out to sea,

By a wind which
is clarity and cool,
and which whips
the yet green trees into
a final leafy dance.

The colossal oak,
which hangs over the
south side of our house,
is raining acorns like stones,
onto the red metal roof
which will save us from
the soon deepening snows.

The noise is sharp and
startling each time,
and they roll in chorus
down to the drowsy ground.
They are the percussive beat
to the hymn which
sings this refrain:
The summer is gone,
summer is really gone.

Paris Revisité

Douzième Anniversaire de Mariage

We arrived back,
twelve years to
the very day,
descending again
from the French
dark while Paris
was still soft in sleep.
The webs of
streetlamps that defined
her luminous essence,
cast black apparitions on
the faces of stilled houses.

We set down our feet
upon her marbled floor,
with no one to notice
but the man from
West Africa, draped
like an ancient king
in greens and gold,
who offered his card.

We sat for our
brief time this time,
and we shared time
as we had then.
We reflected how,
in these moments
and many others since,
life together had become
pan chocolate.
The delicate bread
of our living, cradling
a deep sweetness.

The Satin Man

I knew a man, he was a satin man,
Always sure what he was thinking.
He damned the dirt under his feet,
While his heaven was busy shrinking.

With a mouth that was full of polished stones,
He was careful not to swallow.
Bowed to a savior hung on a crooked tree,
In a cathedral vast and hollow.

The light of day was far too harsh,
For visions captured behind a blindness.
In the dim heart of the hanging judge,
There is no room reserved for kindness.

Fractured light through colored glass,
The chants of death echoed in his ears.
And the images of the tortured saints,
Were washed in their mother's tears.

Gaze far beyond these times we have,
Sacrificing life's days to worry.
The dark's demands have stolen sight,
Here's your grave, but what's your hurry?

Reading Gabriel García Márquez During an Unexpected April Snow

after Having Recently Turned Sixty

Three in
the afternoon,
a timid light
expresses through
the distant grays.
The last
snow of an
unbounded winter,
departs the April day.

The breeze
that follows off
our veiled hills,
is pulling the
white crepe down
from the high limbs.

All around
us, falling fists of
a final wet snow,
punch at the roof
above our heads,
Denting the fresh linen,
dissolving into
the tumble of
the swelling river.

We wonder
how it could have
happened, in a single
night and semi-day,
Between the gates
of a nascent spring.

Then, we agree
to believe a story
that we tell ourselves,
watching a muted sunset
settle in the trees.
It might have
just been a spell,
Cast from the first
dream of old age.

Occam's Razor

for Charles A. Noon III

In cases of ifs, ands, and butting,
Occam's Razor can be quite cutting.

In controversies short and long,
It permits us to simply be wrong.

Do not fear becoming rueful,
When just seeking that which is truthful.

In cases if, or, and maybe,
It is never wise to split a baby.

Leonardo Flies Home

Leonardo Da Vinci took
his place across the tiny isle
from me, and buckled
the belt of his seat.

I was certain it was him.
Too timid to speak,
I listened as he told
the attendant in the
blue-black skirt-suit,
he was returning
from a long overdue visit
with his kid sister in Phoenix.

The New Mexico sun
remained red and settled upon
the bareness of his cheeks.
The layover at Kennedy had
granted him just enough time
to grab a Coke and a slice.

He studied the movements of
her calves carefully as she
trolled ahead in the cabin,
gauging all of the tender
architectures of her sway.
Sketching upon his napkin,
he sipped his orange juice, and
leaned back into a reverie.

Beneath his hair, wiry and limp,
against a raggedy blanket of beard,
I could almost hear the notes of
machines assembling in his head.

The gears and wings, the
rockets and parachutes, the
motions that made the
birds lift skyward, and those
contraptions of battle
that would live to eclipse
horse and sword and shield.

Traipsing the heights of
the atmospheric perspective,
describing Earth's lights reflected
against the cold black of the Moon.

Devoted as I have been to the
celebration of life's soft edges.
I thought to touch his shoulder,
hoping we might speak.

I longed to understand the
miracles of chisel at stone, how the
oily applications of ground pigments,
became lambency and shadow.
The virgin he settled among the rocks.
The tenderness in the eyes of his angels.
The satin cheeks of the Italianate ladies.

The despair of Jerome in his wilderness.
Judas clutching his purse on the wall in Milano.
The mounts of his imagination in pitched battle.

Soon, time again had passed, our dinners arrived,
and I was left to the contentments of flight,
and a wandering, wondering mind.
Below us the ascending cloud mountains,
below them, the dappled cerulean sea.

Last Night's Game

Last night
in a dream,
I was playing
Wiffle Ball, with
Meryl Streep.

She had three
young sons,
who all looked
just like her.
I was pitching,
when one of them
got up to bat.

I served up my
wicked Wiffle curveball.
He drove a shot
to deep left.
Meryl ran it down
like a cat on lightning.

I tried to play
the cut-off but,
Meryl fired that thing
like a cannon,
right to home plate.

The kid was safe anyway.

Simple Summer Poem

The summer river
swells and strains,
The day that follows
the summer rains.

Watching here
I am left to wonder,
At the crack of light
that precedes the thunder.

And my friend the heron
who can naught but wish,
Gazing into the turmoil
that conceals the fish.

The earth, the clouds
and the rain between,
The tailors that drape
the world in green.

Roses

The old women
in New Hampshire
wear their hair just as
they did that day, sitting
still and flushed with the
new greens of spring, that
day the photographer came,
unpacking lens and lights in
the school's shellacked gym,
to snap-capture them in
their pale young essence for a
big book to mark the occasion.

It is still soft-curled, pin-straight,
conformed to braiding, kept
cleanly back with tiny clips,
the silver an inheritance of years.
They wear long denim dresses,
blouses with tiny flowers, maybe
a necklace of strung silver beads,
or colored bits of glass.

They talk through long noontimes
of grandchildren and cats,
their herb garden brimming with
rosemary and mint, behind the house
where their grandmothers were born,
and where the sun has always come
to spend the summer's days.

The shed doors lean now at odd angles,
shedding splinters and petals of old paint.
The rusted trowel still plants the peonies,
the spouted can still carries the water.

They have stayed, and will stay,
the girls they always were,
cleaning strands of past mornings
from the bristles of a favorite brush,
before a mirror they can still
picture as new, roses forever
blooming on the trellis of their youth.

Retornare a Casa

to Giuseppe Tripi

Great-grandfather,
I am here now,
To be what has
become of you.

After the years
of mending nets,
Drawing the life from
this exquisite blue,
Dreams too small were
tossed back to the sea.

Your son left you, left
the steep inclines of
this smoldering rock,
Because the days
were too long, the
life far too short.

But Great Grandfather,
I am here now,
Child of your children's
children's children,

To tell you, I too
cast my nets each day,
Hoping to capture words
that I too will arrange like
fish on this black sand,
That I too hope will
nourish and sustain and,
perchance, become a feast.

A Letter to My Strombolianos

March 2019-Stromboli, Italy

When I could not
find you among the living,
I searched among the dead.
So many names, our names.
Tripi, Famularo, Tesoreiro,
Cincotta, Moleta, and Renda.

Your stones were worn mute,
by the rain and pumice wind.
The slabs and crucifixes fractured,
shaken loose by generations
of sun, soot and tremors.

Even in this paradise, green
with the libretto of creation,
These monuments,
chiseled by a steady hand
and an eternal hope,
have not faired well.

The cameos are worn bare,
the words refuse the reading.
They have become ancient
before their time.

Still, they have left me
a consoling silence,
A resting place for
birds and angels,
where tiny green lizards
can lie and absorb the day.

The volcano that is this place,
continues to murmur and spark.
It holds us, it reminds us,
and it draws us close.

October the Twenty-Eighth

for Gerrit Joost de Jonge

The dark has grown
to overtake the days,

The broad door to November
has cracked open,

The piquant colors of dying
flutter down the empty air.

I awoke in a lingering nighttime,
the dawn nowhere to be found.

Today, winter sent its
first dispatch from the north.

The rains, tonight the winds,
will bring down the choir,

Cupping the river's waters,
bending the trees to its will.

We are here again, centered
in all our familiar.

We will pull back the drapes
and invite the angled light.

In a chilled noon, the sky
is its most noble blue.

We will accept what is left,
and account the days until,

This Earth makes its tilt
toward life's green reiteration.

The Cedar Waxwings

The Cedar Waxwings
like well-sharpened knives,
Cutting the pale breeze
with wheeling and dives.

They found my today
from azurine sky,
Tinctured with rainbows
seducing the eye.

If I could join them
and elude despair,
Dance all their dances
in the river's lair.

Sure, it's one of life's
lamentable things,
Damned by gravity
and yearning for wings.

The Windward Passage

for Per and Ann Blomqvist-Jan 2017

From our sternward berth,
the sea following Queen Elizabeth
has assumed a braided wake.

In our hearing,
the whispered songs
of our long isolations,
the orbiting horizon
ever-steadfast and remote.

Under this sun,
the knotty conflicts of
the roving continents well
behind and beyond,
contained somewhere safe
beneath the hollow sky.

This morning,
the reclining island of Cuba
is a child lying on its back,
searching these tumbling clouds
for faces and circus beasts.

The stories of the turtles
are never revealed, porpoises
gallop in the spilling swells
of afternoons blue and bare.

Yet, in the starry darkness,
we sleep amidst all
the ancient conversations,
of wind and crackling halyards
and the snap of taught canvas.

Beneath this noble Queen,
the briny bones of sailors,
of proud clippers and galleons,
chant their dreams in
crypts of abiding slumber.
We, all but mariners, heading
where the currents convey us.

Theology

We all have our jobs,
Don't we?

Some pick the apples,
some watch them rot
where they lie.

There are those who
carry the water, and those
who cause it to spill.

Some plant trees, and some
use them to build crosses
that will burn the night.

And of course there are those
gifted bomb makers, and the ones
who must become the debris.

In the colliding of holy books,
we have all become soldiers.
And where are the healers
to tend the gaping wounded?

When it is done, and all
the prayers have been uttered,
the sacred candles expired,
We must rise from our knees.

Some of us will die, some
will have to bury the dead.

Ode to a Flat Mouse

Oh mouse, now by my tires pressed,
Treading you surely to thy final rest.

Tiny breaths n'er more serenely drawn,
So cruelly from these fair woods torn.

With mournful words, I your memory serve,
Lo, late too late to break and swerve.

Now, condemned to this eternal grief,
Rueful slumber, torments without relief.

Oh mouse, here lying sprawled and thin,
One last place you ought to not have been.

Dear Honor

It was at eight
this summer morning,
when the news
arrived from Rosserk,
composed into a document
that certified the facts.

Shocking though it was,
too late to mourn,
the years had
erected a wall
tall as Croagh Patrick.

It cast its
leaning shadow,
upon and across the silent
bogs of Ballysakeery, and
over the shoulders
of an ocean that
had come to define,
the what is from the
what might have been.

They left you
behind, far behind,
in the stony fields of
dew and hunger, in a
cramped shanty smelling
of damp and peat.

Now here, in America,
four lifetimes beyond
a dreadful end,
it has become
myself, the first of yours,
to gather these truths.

Honor Moran née Judge,
Mother of Thomas John,
Grandmother of Theodore John,
Great-grandmother of Thomas Daniel, and
Great Great-grandmother of Daniel Thomas.

Honor Moran of Rosserk,
cottier and widow of Thady,
26 July 1905, of age and
debility of four months duration,
and erysipelas of four days duration,
Dead, at aged seventy years,
in the Fever Hospital
of the Ballina Workhouse.

North from Boston

Pay no mind
to the dead.

They know
nothing of leaving,
nothing of lolling
silent in the dirt.

In the dim closet
at the top of our stairs, they
dwell among the smells
of their old clothes.

When the meal
is served, they sit down
in their chair to dine.

While we attempt sleep,
they wriggle and strain
in the bound confines
of picture frames,
emerging with conceit
to attend our dreams.

It's how they prefer it,
lingering in the heads
of the living, in cupboards
with broken latches.

Pay no mind
to the dead.

As they call out
in odd dialects,
their fingers seeming
warm, and their hair
combed in the way
it always was.

Pay them no mind.
They want only what
is theirs. And we,
murmuring to ourselves
in the dark, do not
have it to give.

At Nompondo Village
KwaZulu Natal, South Africa

for Al Basile

Here in Africa,
in the kingdom of Zulu,
the work is unadorned.

The wringing of a mop.
The placing of bundled thatch
against the rain and sun.
The dance of a pencil
on a well-worn schoolbook.

A long solitary walk
down a red-dust road
to fetch the requisites for
an obliging day.
Stirring potatoes and
chicken feet in an old pot.

Brown women pull
browned leaves to
clear space for the new.
The insistent sun
pulls the life from the dirt.
Creatures majestic and concealed
take to the savannah and shade.
Minutes are remembered
as themselves.

The dead lie deep and
the living are their messengers.
Time becomes other,
stars sprayed against the black,
too many to count.

Here amid the work,
there is only this place,
Where the hills have
slept through ages
and the long nights.

They begin and end
each day with a light
that is serene and golden,
and makes the shadows bloom.

In the Kingdom of Autumn

for Desmond Egan

Autumn, I am
fearing I have not
loved you well enough,
Your shrewd airs
and pastel drape,
Your requiems and
gem-spattered nights,
Your numinous
songs of leaving.

You lay with me long,
before my knowing, long
before the gods had died.
You were preaching,
while I sat sleeping in
the space between pews.

Now, missing
what might have
been missed, I
do not need your love,
But only for you
to know of my own.
Desirous of your bony touch,
the wind carries what's lost,
and the scent of coming snows.

Beep

Our new automatic rice
cooker sings to us when
we turn it on.
Our dishwasher sings
when it turns off.

The clothes dryer
declaims in a voice that is
decidedly more aggressive.
It points a gun at our head, and
demands to be emptied. Now.
The laptop, a real free spirit,
chortles all day long for
any number of reasons.

But it is the car I hate,
The car that reminds me of
a wife left behind years ago.
It nags and nags and nags,
with buzzes, beeps and dings,
apprising me of my failures.

Forgetting to latch
my safety belt. Not shutting
the door all the way. Over-
looking an overdue oil change.

It especially loves to let me know
(with an unmistakable glee), that
I've been driving quite long enough
with my turn signal going, all
the other drivers having
already called me an idiot.

I don't mind the chirps that
tell me I am about to be run
down by a truck backing up,
Or the one that clicks to tell
blind people that they can
now safely cross the street.

Even my new hearing aids,
that make it possible for me
to hear all the other electronic things
that niggle and afflict me, feel
they must bleat their tiny melody
straight into my ear when their
battery is about to die.

If they did not, I might not
ever hear all the other beeps,
and jingles and cheerful tinkles.
Would that not be tragically delicious,
especially when served up with
gloppy, overcooked rice?

On a Flight to Boston

I never spoke
to the man beside me
on the plane.
What words spent
could matter to
either of us?

We were leaving home,
or heading home.

There was nothing but
a delusive flatness below.
The insistent sunlight
was nearly painful, and
The gray nothingness
of travel had left our eyes
straining against sleep.

But for three hours
in our two lifetimes,
With elbows in proximity,
knees straining to the fore,
Together, we had defied
the inconspicuous essence
of the universe.

And we soared along the
arbitrary arc of time,
Rising and falling
through clouds, each
embraced by his own
silence.

Saturday Morning in America – 25 November 2017

I awoke slowly
this morning in a
darkness which waited
impatiently for the sun
to find the horizon.

I greeted two cats, I
ground the oily beans
which would become
my coffee, and turned
on the TV to get
the latest revisions of
yesterday's body counts.

Once again it is someone
who prays one way,
who has slaughtered people
who pray another way.

Three more overdoses in
Manchester last night.
the Black Friday shoppers
stampeded at the mall
looking for bargains,
to celebrate the birthday
of The Baby Jesus.

The President was up early,
and has already tweeted
things that would be
an embarrassment even
for a seventh grader
with only half his wits.

This morning, I am grateful
it is only two men,
among 7,548,878,499,
who are threatening to
wipe out life on Earth
before lunchtime.
Tomorrow, thankfully,
The Patriots should
have an easy win
over the Dolphins.

But who will dare
to stand up in defiance
and take a knee?

Robert Frost Repairs a Lamp

That lamp that stands
beside us the night,
Resolved to flicker
left and right.

Disparaging of
my woman's need,
Making it awfully
hard to read.

But as we slept
it mattered naught,
Within that time whence
dreams are wrought.

To fair lady's desire
I finally bended,
Lamp's flickering days
Now finally ended.

The Marble Merchant of Jabalpur

On that dust and stone hill
high above the Marble Falls,
the marble merchant squatted
the way men squat in India,
bottom against the dirt
knees pressed to shoulders.

Beneath his tarpaulin,
five wooden shelves
featuring his store of stones,
each a proper fit for
the palm of a man.

I considered him and
I considered his stones.
He studied me as well, in that
way a man studies a man
who has something to offer.

One by one he proffered each,
writing on his open palm
the price of them. First
one hundred-fifty rupees, then
one hundred, then seventy-five.

After we had our dance,
I chose the one which
spoke to me with the
clearest voice, and then
handed him 150 rupees,

Agreeing as we must that,
in consideration of fine rocks,
between men of will and willing,
One should not quarrel long,
or fail to strike the bargain,
over an issue of fifteen pennies.

Here,

in New Hampshire,
the now is
only soon.

Hours take their leisure.
The mountains feel
no need to stand
to greet the sun.

The rivers move
in the manner of
rain slipping down
a pane of glass.
The air possesses
nothing but the light.

It is very different
from the place
of my birth,
New York City,
where seconds
are gemstones,
and life is stacked
upon itself.

Here,
I can be a man
whose horizon
is tucked behind
a hill, a man
who tries each day
to sing the clocks
to slumber.

A man who listens
when the dark asks,
for me to carry
my love to sleep.

A man who wakes
her gently, when
the early glints,
reach out across
the tree tops.

The Man across the River

The man across
the river collects
history, and sticks.
He assembles them
into stacks, and
into paragraphs.

We have
spoken about it,
now and again.
We have noticed
those things fallen,
those yet standing.

There are
those things
that defy the
long hurtle of time,
Those things crumbling
and decaying, and
crackling and snapping
beneath our footsteps.

There are
the things that
we determine
to tell others, and
things we must
keep close.
The trees
keep reaching until
they can no longer.

Men like us,
men like the man
across the river,
men like me, are
just the same.

We can
be content spending
lifetimes wondering
what is there high
over the blue treetops,
what is just beneath
the heaped litter.

And when it has
all been uttered,
when all our stories
have fallen behind us,
We admire the
reticence of boulders,
and the endless
dispassionate travels
of water.

Tiger Hunting with Gregg Allman Last Night

I don't hunt and
I've never met Gregg Allman.
But, in the dream
I was hunting
with Gregg Allman.

We had
to climb to the top
of a big mountain.
We were hunting
for tigers.
We had no guns.
Gregg only had a
nasty-looking knife.

Our guide,
who had no face,
instructed us
to lie on the ground
back to back.
He said to stay still,
the tigers would come.

They did.
About half a dozen.
And they all
laid down beside me,
and Gregg Allman,
and the guide with no face.

We made like we
were asleep.
Gregg Allman was ready
with the nasty knife.

Then the guide
with no face shouted,
"Now!"

He said that
Gregg Allman should
stab the closest tiger,
right in the jugular.
So he did.

The Tiger was not happy.
He reeled around and
he staggered around,
bleeding out of his neck
until he was dead.
The other tigers ran off.

Then, we all went
into a little house,
maybe the little house of
the guide with no face.
He never said.
We took off our shoes,
and sat for a nice
cup of tea.

I could not help but
notice, that Gregg Allman
had apparently also
stabbed something that
looked like a beaver
which was lying there,
in a heap with a
hole in its neck,
dead as a doornail
on the little house floor.

I took a sip of tea,
and I wondered.....
This is my dream.
Where the hell was I
when that happened?

Reading on the Porch on the Last Day of Summer

for David McCullough

Once again, there is the door
which is this book, held like a
small bird against my open palms,
a prayer of wandered meditation.

Once again, embraced by a spell,
into time with no timepieces,
I am hearing the musings of
a wind through a cornfield.

I sense that swirling anxiety
of compelling passion, tracing
a finger along the bared creases
of another man's map.

Humming along with the trilling birds,
glasses touching glasses at
a fine party, a raised arm waving
farewell from the window of a train.
The story being told is about
a man who tells stories.

At once something stirs me back,
back from far and contented travels,
whistle-stops on the well-worn
outlying edges of the possible,
to find that these trees have
been awaiting me in silence.

The concentric gossamer threads of
an orb weaver, sways weightless
in angled light and a feeble breeze.

What I had not heard, I hear now.
The limpid voices of home, all
that is faithful and familiar, and
the river swaying, still singing.

Obituaries

The dead people
in
the Sunday Paper
are always
smiling,
Alive in
some carefree
moment when
someone had
the thought to
snap
a quick shot.

The photo is
always
from a day
long past,
When
their hair was
thick with waves,
Their eyes winning
and lit with the
blind luminescence
of ten million hopes.

For those of us
who never knew them,
sitting quiet
under the blush
of a Sunday lamp,
This is
who they are,
Just how we will
always recall them.

Accumulations

I surround myself
with familiar things.
Things collected for
no good reason.
Things which take up
the empty spaces in a life.
Things which reassure and
remind me of where
I have been, who I am.

One day in 1961,
when I was about four,
my Mother saved two
hands full of bits she
found in my pockets.
Things found during
a boyhood day which
seemed important,
even useful, too good
to leave languishing
among the overlooked.

A button, a toy soldier,
a small spring, and nine
things with no name.

Nothing has been
changed by time.
Everything has a meaning,
that I have assigned, and
a name I have given it.
My pockets are still
filled each day, emptied
into the pages of books.

Someday, soon after
my leaving, and
just as I had done,
my children will wander
among these walls and
over these floorboards,
and gaze at it all.

They will wonder what
it was I was thinking, and
realize just how much,
will remain as riddle.
Then they will hire a man,
who drives an old truck,
to come and take it all away.

The Sheriff

This morning, there
is a new Sheriff
on my TV screen,
struggling in the
bright lights, backed up
against the darkness.

Before a bank of
microphones he is
struggling to answer
all the questions,
of where and when,
how many dead
this time? Did they
get the shooter?

He is describing
the familiar scene, of
chaos and strewn bodies,
people running for exits,
hiding in bathroom stalls,
silent and screaming.

The Sheriff,
had not told his wife
that tonight he might
be out all night.
It will take time
to sort it all out, to
locate and gently inform
the next of kin.

We will need
to be patient.
The investigation
will take time, if
he is to do it right.
He reminds us that
victims deserve that.

In the coming days,
The Sheriff will
live in our living rooms.
The Sheriff's name
will be spoken a
thousand million times.
Then we will all
forget this Sheriff,
forever.

The Sixties

These are the days
once dreamed, years ago
when our bodies were
flush with youth,
minds still germinating,
Preoccupied by
a muted discontent,
longing for things we
could not yet describe.

Now, in the forest
of lingering afternoons,
we read until the words
draw our lids down
upon themselves,
Bodies nested, and
half upright in
a favored chair.

We sleep in the
hushed company of cats,
who lie curled upon
chosen pallets of sun,
fur like fields of rye.
They know nothing
of time nor desire,
neither do they
doubt the days past,
nor fear those ahead.

When we seem willing,
They teach us
what they can.

Back on The North Fork of Long Island

for Bob and Ginny Blank

Many years now gone by,
this horizon remains familiar.
The long east-west paths I
wore down smooth and thin,
along shoreline drawn between
these tender swells of sand
and the great Metropolis,
scenes where Einstein
and Whitman played.

There are the hamlets where
I courted love and failure,
where I cradled the babies,
places I sang harmony with the
Paumanok songs of Murray
and Everett and Planz,
places where I laid my head, and
stretched out a careworn back.

Fence following fence and
hedge following hedge,
turnoffs to one beach
after the next, where live
the Sound breezes on which
gulls would glide and knife.

Still the ghosts of potato farms,
now miles of grapevines, shoulders
strung over wires on locust posts.
That rusted tractor has still
not turned its wheels, nested there
along the old North Road which
seems to have just one last rise,
one more bend before the last.

Again, as in the profuse and
distant Spring days before me,
the buds are beginning to
express their desires, and
the sky is, as was ever so,
a sumptuous blue arc.

It has been a long nine years
since our leaving, imagining
a green future among mountains
and rivers and towns whose
paths and pastures were foreign,
whose names we did not know.

But here, along this finger of strand,
on this island dense with faces
and not so distant recollections,
nothing has changed, but me.

Elegy for *Homo sapiens*

Like the
warships
they
worshipped,
They fell
prey to the
squalls.

Lifted
banners
on
borders,
Guards on
garrison
walls.

Like their
gods and
their
gardens,
That were
destined to
wilt.

They could
never
be
perfect,
As the
weapons they
built.

Being at Sea

On The Queen Victoria, June 2018

At sea,
time dilates,
Waves, moments
passing fore to aft.

The dawns
force themselves,
Up from
the black distance.

The dusk suns
drop as a pearl,
Into a glass
of champagne.

And, as ever
the wind has
Its way, over
the ancient depths.

Skittles and a Sacred Vision

On the flight to Miami,
the little nun beside me
offered some of her Skittles
from a tiny zip-lock that
was nested in her vestments.

She explained that she was
a Capuchin Sister of Nazareth.
Wrapped in faded brown muslin, a
simple white rope round her waist was
all she needed to hold her together.

She spoke chapter and verse,
of her sisters around the world,
members of the army of
St. Francis of Assisi, women
who had, as girls, forsaken both
the world and womanhood
for a devotion to an unlikely tale.

She was on her way to Bolivia,
to a village in a jungle clearing,
Determined to bring Jesus
and the fear of damnation to
a school of tiny brown-faced souls.

High above the Carolina clouds,
it was clear that she had taken
no vow of silence.
She continued to talk,
without pause or acts of mercy,
until I thought to feign sleep.

Then, she popped a few Skittles,
and opened her iPad for the mute,
piquant devotions of solitaire.

Among the Wounded

Some things are solved only by sleep,
some things are solved by morning.
A pestering past squanders the day,
arriving with no warning.

The cloaked alleys of our sadness,
were established in the child.
Lingering long through life's laments,
they refuse to be exiled.

New Hampshire

They came north, to this
kingdom of stone and frost,
Felling trees the size of ships
to make splinters for shelter.

Harnessing the muscle
of great of beasts,
to drag stone and stump,
and scratch at the ground,
Stacking their obstacles
one over the next,
they patterned the meadows
and enclosed their hopes.

They begged sun and water,
coaxed what they could
from the unmerciful dirt,
Before the days grew short,
and New England autumn
lit the hills in savage light.

Among all living things, they
learned to abide the winters that
entombed the hills and hollows
in the whitest of silences.

Now, coursing along roadsides,
their walls stand as memory,
Tumbled by trees, split
by ice and thaw and ice,
In shade and in sunlight,
soft-greened with moss.

The woods now speckled
with stone cellar holes,
collapsing under the slow
and certain burden of time.
Here their homes stood, and
their sturdy, steadfast hearts
battled the marching forest.

This murmuring river
I hear, they too heard.
This slivered silver luster
I ponder, they too pondered.
And now, as then
these abiding stars, drape
the lingering nights, in dreams.

Palika Bazaar

New Delhi, India – January 2013

This, our final day
in Delhi, the air
over the Palika Bazaar
has filled my lungs
with steel wool.

Every step, a man
with things to ply.
The small boy with
strings of tiny beads
presses us for ten rupees.

On the ruddy street tiles,
men with raspy brooms move
dust from place to other place.
A well draped-woman
with a plump baby, begs of
the white faced strangers.

It has been said by some,
the Hindus worship
a thousand gods.
Here on Janpath Street
there is but one god,
Folded in half in
the pockets of tourists.

Shopkeepers chant
mantras, to coax
the god from his temple.

Distracted

I have become the sum
of my distractions.
Paper and ivory, reeds and metal,
taut skins and splinters of wood,
Books that sleep in wait of me.

I whittle elegant places to sit.
I speak a foreign tongue with
no one foreign to reply.
I make music no one will hear.

My eyes do not focus
as they once had, so
I choose what I see, I
rise early and sleep too soon.

My feet tell of my traveling.
My shoulders and knuckles talk to me,
about their memory of work.
I try to not dwell on aches.

I am done with many things.
Many things are done with me.

There will always be
the twigs the storm dropped,
and the battle with the
advancing woods.

I no longer contemplate sunsets.
Mornings rouse me in darkness,
that I may be witness to the rise
of light from the earth.

Always, the survivors will be
the doubt and misgivings,
walking in and out of
the doors to my house.

And after the lights are out
and the doors locked, braiding
themselves into my dreams.

The Wind

We will always
recall days when
a phone would ring.

Death, seeming again
near enough to touch.
The sound of it
becoming the scent,
its apparitions hanging
over us in the trees.

It seems the nature
of this brittle living.
Rooms must be bared,
memory slipped into
a pocket over the heart.

As the sojourn continues,
it lives in our sleep and
navigates through our dreams.
Neither starlight nor dawn
can eclipse that night.

And yet, if we are
willing to embrace it,
it teaches the true reach
of a moment, and the
wealth in a single breath.

The Inception of May

The benumbed
waters born of
the Northland snows, now
receded into the spring,
The venerable rocks
of the Warner River begin
to express themselves.
Stretching from beneath
the cloak of winter,
they order the river's course.

In the newborn light,
my eyes comb the trees
for the familiar, the friends
who had left us here alone,
to contend with the
long and lifeless winter.
Now returned, they
enjoin us to redress,
and to recommence.

Here, together once more,
we await the greening
which will define the
summer's shadows, soften
and festoon the stones,
Contented in the days, and
the budding and leafing
of our common, explicit
hereafter.

Charlottesville

Out there,
America is burning,
Fires rekindled
in dry brush from
the old embers of
torches, once used
for light.

From the shackled hills
of the storied west,
to the scarred valleys
of envisaged horizons,

From the spired
clapboard churches,
to the valleys of
immigrant towns,
where the solemn
courthouse stands vacant
beside the village square.

Last night the people
once again warmed
themselves by the glow
of burning hatred, their
faces lit with fury,
jeering in chorus at
our moribund virtue.

Tomorrow, preachers
will ascend their pulpits,
and invoke the claims
of silent gods while
the people, entitled
by their common fear,
will gather and sing
rich, remembered hymns
in praise of a lost cause.

Sfumato

It is what Leonardo
called *sfumato*,
the smoke.
Life best
depicted
in soft edges,
unbound by pro-
nounced delineations.

The visage of
his mistresses.
The seduction by
his young lovers
in their curled tresses,
the turn at the neck,
the tender folds.

In rocky edges,
blurred by
a tender focus.
The waters, the
mountains, the
distance in the eyes.
Even in the
imagined murmurs
of their lips.

La misura del mondo,
in the *allongé*
of his shadows.
All things emerging
as one, and
nothing but
the imagination,
to perfuse the spaces
between.

Regarding Existence

In this life, don't
let them convince you
that anything is holy,

That there is
something which lives
behind the darkness.

There are no Holy Men,
none who can understand
more than a curious man.

Beware the vestments
of privilege, garments
that conceal a frail logic.

There are no miracles.

There is only a certainty,
that things will happen,
either this way, or that.

Put no faith in power.
Power is only something,
clutched by the fearful.

Don't insist that,
a question begun with why,
must have a reply.

There are things which
can never be known.
They are just as they are.

There is neither destiny,
nor truth to be realized
beyond perishability itself.

If there is a peace
to be granted us,
it is born in this:

In the matter of
this living of ours, All
that needs to be known

is that there is
a radiance, and then
there is none.

While you are yet able,
turn your face to it.

Introduction to Romance

How far away the stars seem
and how far is our first kiss
and ah, how old my heart.

W.B. YEATS

The first girl
who ever kissed
me was fourteen.

So was I.

It was one
afternoon, in the
hallway of McKenna
Junior High School,
when there was no

one else around.

As I recall it,
through the mist
of my drying years,
She had just
walked up and
kissed me, right

on the lips.

Then, the
school year ended,
and she moved away.
That is how it goes

sometimes, with love.

I don't even
have a *selfie* of us.
No one did then.
But I have
something better.

I can remember.

There once was
a pretty girl,
who wanted to
kiss me, and

she did.

The Window

In my head
are many rooms.
A bed with the linens
tossed by sleep.
A table where
a meal will be waiting.
The chair which
holds me best.
The gentle scent of
coffee and new flowers.

In my rooms
are many walls,
papered with the photos
of long dead antecedents.
A wedding day
one hundred years gone.
My Great-grandmother, as
a toddler on her father's knee.
A poem written
in a prior life.

The air is damp with
the mist of the many lines
I have written, and
the ghosts of those
which yet evade me.
The air I breathe is
sweet and familiar.

And there is a window,
a pale curtain half-drawn,
where I can lean, and
call on the world.
I watch the flutter
of a luscious song in
a grand tree which
guards my roof.

The light is alive.
It is another season.
Time is a young lover.

On The Occasion of the Funeral of Donald Hall

at South Danbury, New Hampshire 30 June 2018

Praise be to the men
who find their place
and are content there,

Who understand the
treasures of silence
and small things,

Who can sing with echoes
and make their harmonies
along the wrinkles of time.

And praise be to the men
who press flowers into books
for strangers to find
long after they are gone.

Salvation

Everything
in this forest must
collapse.

Leaf begets earth.
Fruit begets spawn.
Branches splinter.

The rot of trunks
becomes peat.
The thing, its parts.

Stumps become nurse
to saplings and moss.

Stones are concealed
until roots and rain
unveil them again.

The forest falls
and falls in on
itself, nourished by
the long exhalations
of what's dead.

Deeds done by dew
and the invisible.

And then there is
this poem which
unearthed itself on the
road to the landfill.

Written with a pen
fished from the muddle
beneath the car's seat,

It bloomed upon
an envelope,
redeemed from the
recycling bin, that

I hope will
survive to tell.

Boating Through Jabalpur's Marble Canyon

We were eight
in a blue-rusty boat,
rowed slowly through
the up river canyons
of the Marble Falls, pulled
by three pair of slight men,
and another who pointed out
details in the stone cascades.

High on a ledge, a small boy,
and a smaller one as well,
yelled to us words that became
lost among their echoes.
The guide said one of the boys
would jump into the river
for 20 rupees (a nickel).

Thoughtfully, the offer
was considered, then
I said, *Tell them both
to jump.*

Life Savings

Aging is the bank
which accepts deposits,
and will not ever
give them back.
But it does have its
tiny catalogue of
compensations.

I recall those
ancient days when
opening that account
might earn you a new
toaster or blender,
a set of steak knives.

This week, after
finding out that the
the steamy apparition,
which has taken up
residence near the foul pole
in the left field of my vision
is not a brain tumor,

Has made me
oddly less concerned
about how much easier
it seems to be for me
to peer onto my scalp
through the last efforts of
what use to be a magnificent
head of wavy hair.

Much like the sharp January day
I lost my feet on the ice
and knocked myself out cold,
After the nice young doctor
let me know that the brick walk
had not, in fact, cracked my
skull open like a walnut,

I felt a curious pleasure
in knowing that my dear wife
could drive me to the doors
of the local Emergency Room
without killing us both
in a fiery car wreck.

So this afternoon, watching
a great parade of cumulus clouds
as the minutes click off unattended,
I am content in the knowledge
that I will probably not
die this week, or the next.

And accepting of the fact
that today's aches will be
more tolerable today than
they will be tomorrow,
One day I will place my
last nickel in the bank's
cold and stingy metal slot.

I will appeal to some burly nurse
in a flowered top to prop
up my pillow just a bit, and
comb back neatly the gathering
of my last remaining hairs.

But alas, I now proclaim,
In this part of the known world,
it is a few good turns past five
on a pleasing Friday afternoon.
I think I will softly push
the hair back over my head,
and mark the occasion with a
proper toast to my ladylove
and to my good health.

What Color is Blue?

There are
those strands
of our reality
Which defy our
words.

Limply, they
render answers,
Which simply
refuse
to appease.

I thought that
I knew blue,
Until I chanced
to sail on the
Mediterranean.

Now the bluest
of skies only
disappoints.
It makes me blue
to think about it.

Trapped in
the cage
of our senses,
All is but
air and light,

In a sea of
things which
move inside us,
In colors we are
unfit to describe.

To a Man Who Was My Father

28 April 2019

The day they buried you,
I stayed away,
in a place safe
and far removed.

This morning, I
went out to wander,
among the lenient slopes,
Which cradle a place
that is my home.

It was that time, to
remove the leaves that
had succumbed last fall,
Collect the twigs, shaken
loose by the callous winds
of a long winter.

Such sweet toil
is essential, to clear
for spring's children,
a path to their paradise.

An Accomplished Day

Today I saw
the last of last night,
take the moon
off to sleep, while
the sunlight leaned itself
against the river's falls.

I picked up
a green turtle
by the side of
the road and returned
it to the green forest.

I saw
a conference of
three fat whistle pigs
debating beside the road,
clouds carrying rain,
and white ones in
a very blue sky.

I stood in
a glistening meadow
of Orange Hawkweed
and Marsh Marigold,
White Wood Aster and
Blue Flag Iris.

I was there
to see the black
bear cross the road
just beyond me, and
then wander content
down its ambling path.

I turned in time
to see the Great
Blue Heron catch
a rainbow fish and wrestle
it slowly into its belly.

I felt the fish's struggles,
as the Heron bent
to sip of waters which
pooled before falling,
passing beyond my view.

Today. Should you care.
For what it is worth.
Was a good day.

The 5th of July

It is the Tuesday
of a newborn summer.

The sky lies heavy
with sun,
Great crescendos of cloud
tumble at every horizon.

The day lilies along
the roadsides,
Are a gathered choir
that sways in a pale breeze.

The holiday of summer
now past,
Countryside and shore
can reassume their poise.

On days such
as these,
We wander the lanes
of summers past,

The still swings in
vacant schoolyards,
Recalling the scents of
lovers and seashore.

In the rain's music,
in the gambol of time,
in the light of long days,
and an afternoon reflection,

We can almost
call into our mind,
just how young
it all once was.

Sundays

I would like
to have back all
the Sunday mornings
of my childhood.

The tight collars and the
tugging ties,
the parted hair and
pitch-polished shoes,
the broken sleep.

I want back
the hours on my knees,
the nightmares of tormented
saviors and saints.
I want to marvel at
the sharp light of the sun
before it was splintered by
panes of stained glass.

I gave what was asked.
I recited from memory.
I made the pleas for mercy
for all of the awful sins
of my straining youth.

It has been four ages since
I stepped from those pews,
Closed tightly the curtains
to block out the night.

But I can
still hear the bells,
Still see the shadows of
saints in the hanging light.
I can still smell
the incense burning.

Amsterdam

April 2014

In Amsterdam,
we consult two maps.
Ambling the half-moons
of narrow lanes and
still water, we
step aside for the
trams and foot traffic, the
streaming of bicycles that
roll the city's veins.

We stare deeply into
canvas stalls of tulips
and buckets of bulbs,
Shops of warm drink
and pretty sweets.
At Rembrandt's house,
the colors are still ground
on a slab of stone,
linseed added by the drop.

In Amsterdam,
we are the elders, against
an old city decorated
with bloom and beauty.
Young girls talk, eating
sugar-dusted pancakes
festooned with chocolate.
Black coffee clings to the
inclines of porcelain cups.

Two minutes after seven,
the darkness draws aside
the heavy drape of day.
The air becomes fragrant,
a canal's water becomes onyx.
The candied ladies, framed
in their tall windows,
emanate a ruby light.

In Amsterdam, under
the tender sheets of evening,
love comes installed a
quartered hour at a time.
Anyone's dreams might
come true.

To You Who Are Young

Seventeen more dead at Parkland

If you have not yet
come to realize it,
this time is your time.
We of the Baby Boom,
gray, in Dockers and Spanx,
have done our best,
done what we could.

We burned all the
tickets to war along with
our bridges and brassieres,
Insisted that what
appeared different
in us all was,
in fact, the same.
We cleaned the
rivers and cities and
preserved the songbirds
to their green places.

We gave our children
the moon and microchip,
Made a priest of the artist
and an exile of the priest.
We cured your disease.

Still, in our deepest heart,
We know we have failed you.
We saw what needed to be done,
got fat, and then forgot.

But here is the thing.
Posterity will judge us all
for all those many things
we did and did not do.
You too will be judged
by your children, and by
their children, and theirs.

So put down your god-
damned life-killing phones,
and prepare to fight.
It will take that and more.

The sons of bitches
who still rule this world,
have not gone away at all.
They wish to keep you
weakened and ignorant and
confused, and they have gotten
even better at all the miserable,
killing, destroying things they do.

This human existence will
one day come to an end.
No one can stop it.
For the love of all that
has worth in this world,
Get out there and
slow it down.

Here, in the Afterlife

We each keep those things to ourselves,
the long midnights which followed
days behind a locked door.

We contain the pain of our engagements,
the hollow aches, the tightened scars,
the memory left behind in a severed limb.

We had always been nomads without tribe,
walking the dunes in our heart,
believing the promise of our mirages.

Silently we marked the dates in our head,
stepping cautious around the ditches
so as to not to slip or be swallowed.

We each lived through the many days
knowing the many and not the other,
believing one day we would meet us.

We imagined a kingdom of tall trees
staying green through winters,
set over hills where snow came to sleep.

We imagined the syllables of water
chanting its *berceuse* in the darkness,
lighting upon our peculiar forever.

And Once Again, November

What shall we do
in this slowing of clocks?
in this lengthening darkness?

The noble pines and sky
have bended, folding us
into an early sleep.
The sun has stolen off
with the apples of October.

The bark is blackened,
the stone wall blackened,
abandoned by the leaving light.
The constellations emerge
and bewilder the weary.

Soon it will be
a deepening cold and
frost songs at the morning.

From ice clouds
the snows will arise
to make it all silver.

We will begin to
know the word *home*,
in the way we came
to know our lover's eyes.

The New Hampshire winter
will pose its riddle, and
then give us the gift of
stillness, and of staying put.

Visitations

I love the world,
when it does not
encroach,
When people
do not knock
at my door.

I want to know
what is happening,
out there
between commercials.
I want to worship,
but I find
nothing sacred.

So I am contented
with bottomless thinking
about the
blossom of daylight,
and the complexion
of the darkness.

I roll it around,
forcing it into
the deep corners
of my skull.

Here and there
I feel inspired
to sing, and then I
retreat again to silence.

Come find me,
but don't stay long.
There are things
I need to get back
to not doing.

There are passages
and the past
to contemplate.
Dedicating myself to
those places where
I can feel free,
to be lost and chanting
at the stillness.

Dylan Goes Domestic

You really are the best Bob,
sometimes I must agree,
You got yourself a one true love
but Babe, It Sure Ain't Me.

Maybe you could pick up your socks,
while you are pickin' out that new song.
If you could take out the garbage once,
Bob, would that really be so wrong?

The Times They Are A Changin',
isn't that exactly what you said?
How about putting down the Tambourine Man,
and go in and make the bed.

I really never bought that crap
about how you're Like a Rolling Stone,
Maybe one time you might walk the dog,
maybe even once answer the phone.

There are dishes piled in the sink,
And the stink is getting strong,
If you could stop being Dylan for a day,
Bob, would that be so wrong?

The last thing that you bought for me
a silly Leopard Spot Pillbox Hat.
How about doing something real exotic, Bob
maybe go in and feed the cat.

Sure, your road will stay Forever Young
no matter how old and creased you are.
While you're out revisiting Highway 61
how about gassing up the car?

When the crowds all cheering you, Bob
who's stuck here in this prison?
It's me who's Tangled Up in Blue,
while you're out busy being Dylan.

On The Queen Elizabeth – May 2015

for Stewart and Elizabeth Wilson

From her stout prow
that bisects this headwind,
the sky is a cathedral.
The sea belies direction.

Here and again, the gray
has tipped open a blue window.
The place where my heart resides
holds a book on her palms.

I am thoroughly vanished
in the words of a man
named Gabriel García Márquez.
His words are seabirds that
soar and dance the wind.

They humble me, just as
the sea humbles me, within
the sky's endless deep.

And then is the lesson,
floating within the joys
of an exquisite emptiness.
How small is one man,
even a man in love.

The Life Well-Lived

Truth is,
all of life's
desires,
are
bad for you.

Some are
especially bad.

Ice cream and handguns.
Staying up late.
Whiskey and free love.

Steaks and loud music.
Sitting in chairs.
Butter and psychedelics.

Speed and devotion.
Breathing in cities.
Sunshine and salt.

It's all about
just what
you can
resist, and
for how long.

And who's
keeping count?

I say,
swing hard
and don't forget
to touch
all the bases.

To the Woman at the Party Last Night Who Just Had to Bring It Up

Don't think that I don't get your point.
Even if it makes no sense at all, it
was still well articulated.
Perhaps it was how you offered it.
Like a platter of delicate tastes
with a bit too much curry.
If I try, I can see things your way.
You know I want to, but
it feels like I'm forcing my foot
into a shoe which is ill-fitted,
like sleeping in someone else's bed.
After all, we are all humans,
each of our skulls slightly misshapen,
and filled with such separate thoughts,
Each of us fighting back the overgrowth
along the course of our chosen path.
But please, consider re-thinking it all
and I pledge to do the same.
We can agree that it's only fair, then
having given both opinions fair chance,
at least one of us will be certain,
that you were completely wrong.

DANIEL THOMAS MORAN, born in New York City in 1957, earned a Baccalaureate in Biology from Stony Brook University in 1979 and a Doctorate in Dental Surgery from Howard University in 1983. He is the author of eleven previous collections of poems which include *Here in the Afterlife* (Integral Contemporary Literature Press/Romanian translation by Lidia Vianu (The University of Bucharest, 2017), *A Shed for Wood* (2014, Salmon Poetry), *Nieve de Agosto y otros poemas* (Diaz Grey Editores/ Spanish translation by Mariela Dreyfus, New York University, 2014), *Looking for the Uncertain Past* (Poetry Salzburg, 2006), *From HiLo to Willow Pond* (Street Press, 2002), and *In Praise of August* (Canio's Editions, 1998).

His poems and essays have appeared in such publications as *The New York Times, The Humanist, Columbia Journal, Confrontation, Commonweal, Contemporary Literature Review India, Exit 13, Hawaii Pacific Review, The Guardian, Hektoen International, iManhattan, Instanbul Literature Review, The Journal of The American Medical Association, Levure Litteraire, Literary Matters, Medical Humanities Journal, Nonad's Choir, Nassau Review, Opium, Poetry Salzbug Review, Prairie Poetry, Rattapallax, The Recorder, Sfera Eonica, The Journal of Dental Humanities, Street Magazine, The Seventh Quarry, Like Light: 25 Years of Poetry and Prose* (Bright Hill Press), *New Contrast: South Africa Literary Journal* and *VIA:Voices in Italian Americana* (Bordighera Press).

He was appointed Poet Laureate by The Legislature of Suffolk County, NY in 2005, and was Vice-President of The Walt Whitman Birthplace Association. His collected papers are being archived in The Dept. of Special Collections of The Frank Melville, Jr. Library at Stony Brook. He is also Chairman of The Dean's Advisory Board for The University Libraries at Stony Brook. He has collaborated with artists worldwide as part of the Austria based Password Project and also in collaboration in *The Ekphrasis Project* with artist Gerrit Joost de Jonge of The Netherlands. He has been an ordained Humanist Minister since 2005 and is presently Arts Editor for *The Humanist* magazine in Washington, D.C.

After being in the private practice of dentistry for twenty-six years, and five years teaching, in 2013 he retired as Clinical Assistant Professor from Boston University's School of Dental Medicine, where he twice earned national awards for Excellence in Clinical Teaching. In 2011, he was honored by being selected to deliver the School of Dental Medicine's Commencement Address. In 2019, he was honored by being asked to read a poem of his at the inauguration of New Hampshire Governor Chris Sununu. In addition, Dr. Moran is a skilled maker of Windsor Chairs. He and his wife Karen live on The Warner River in Webster, New Hampshire.

Photograph: Karen K. Moran

salmonpoetry

Cliffs of Moher, County Clare, Ireland

"Like the sea-run Steelhead salmon that thrashes upstream to its spawning ground, then instead of dying, returns to the sea—Salmon Poetry Press brings precious cargo to both Ireland and America in the poetry it publishes, then carries that select work to its readership against incalculable odds."

TESS GALLAGHER

The Salmon Bookshop & Literary Centre

Ennistymon, County Clare, Ireland

"Another wonderful Clare outlet."
The Irish Times, 35 Best Independent Bookshops